Saying "No" to Negativity

Saying "No" to Negativity

*How to Manage Negativity
in Yourself, Your Boss,
and Your Co-Workers*

Zoie Kaye

*SkillPath Publications
Mission, Kansas*

Project Editor: Kelly Scanlon

Editor: Jane Doyle Guthrie

Cover Design: Rod Hankins

Book Design: Rod Hankins and Premila Malik Borchardt

ISBN: 1-57294-017-4

Library of Congress Catalog Card Number: 95-73270

20 19   09 08 07 06

Printed in the United States of America

People can alter their lives by altering their attitudes.

—William James

Contents

one

What Causes Negativity?

Are your family members negative?

Are your co-workers negative?

Are you working for an operation that has an overall negative attitude?

The attitudes of those around us can have a tremendous impact on our own. "Attitude" encapsulates the way we look at and react to situations because of our mind-set. Someone who views life through dark-colored glasses may actually go on to experience or cause negative events. We all know people who appear to go through life with a black cloud hanging over them—"Nothing ever works out right for me," they moan and complain. "Something always goes wrong."

If you're spending a lot of time around a person or group that gives off predominately negative "vibes," you may be surprised to realize the impact this can have on your own attitude. Learning to recognize negativity before you become a part of it can have a big effect on your own outcomes. Negativity is nothing to dismiss lightly—it can affect your health, your productivity, and, very importantly, your happiness.

What explains how something so destructive can take over so many people? Well, one major culprit is change, which exerts external influence on our attitudes, and the other source is our basic, "deep down" outlook toward life, which is a powerful internal influence.

The Effects of Change

Have you noticed all the changes taking place in your work environment? Some make big waves; others are more subtle. Nothing, however, appears to be constant. Not more than a generation or so ago an individual would work for the same company for thirty or forty years and then be honored with a gold watch on retiring. That's definitely a thing of the past— multiple careers in a lifetime have now become the norm. Technology has increased the speed at which changes occur in both our professional and our personal lives. A confident "we've always done it this way" is no longer an appropriate reference point; a prerequisite for today's job market is *flexibility*. An employee currently must be willing to accept change and maintain a good attitude in order to survive.

Let's examine some of the changes of the past few years in both our professional and our personal lives.

Professional Environment

Teams. Frequently these days the once independent worker is asked to step into a position of interdependence—to be a *team player*. This paradigm shift has created chaos in many organizations. Often those hardest hit are employees who have long performed the same routine, repetitive job under the direction of a very "hands on" manager and are now asked to make decisions, problem solve, increase their interpersonal skills, and sometimes even cross-train with their team members. Imagine the resistance and fear (and *negativity*) these workers may feel.

Also noticeably affected are middle managers, who in the past felt secure in their authority and hierarchical positions and now are being asked to train former subordinates to do their jobs. This leaves middle managers wondering if they will have a job when the process is complete. These managers may feel that they're losing the control and power base they've spent years building. New rules and uncertainty have become the norm, which is stressful and conducive to negativity.

Downsizing. Downsizing can create great pressure and uncertainty for employees. For example, support staff who formerly assisted one person may now be attempting to satisfy the needs of five or six different bosses. The pressure on these employees to maintain their previous level of job performance ultimately affects their attitude, productivity, and physical health. A slide into negativity is not far off when people are asked to perform duties for which they have no skills and no appropriate training.

Personal Environment

Family life. Two incomes have become a necessity for many families in order to meet the needs of educating and supporting children. Directly related to this, child care is a major concern to working parents. Workers who are moving across the country as a result of transfers or in search of new opportunities no longer have the family network available to assist them with child care and other household issues. With the rise of crime in so many neighborhoods, youngsters often can't go home and play with friends until their parents return from work. And the increasing accessibility of drugs to all ages makes home life even more difficult for many families.

Sandwich generation. The pressures of moving into the "sandwich generation" can take a toll on middle-aged people. Reabsorbing grown children who have returned home unable to support themselves and caring for elderly parents who require supervision and financial assistance can be emotionally, financially, and physically draining, thus leaving members of this sandwich generation vulnerable to a sagging attitude.

Racial and sexual inequality. True equality is still lagging in many areas and for many people. Many appropriate-sounding words are tossed around today, but statistics and personal experience often don't bear out real advances in achieving racial and sexual equality. In both the personal and business arenas, this *lack* of change is straining relations in an already stressful environment.

Financial pressures. Men and women have to work harder than ever today to make ends meet. Young people are completing college and entering the workforce now with large education loans to repay, sapping their incomes for perhaps ten years or more after they graduate. Parents can't necessarily count on being able to provide their children with all the essentials, much less "luxuries" such as family vacations. These frustrations can nourish the seeds of negativity into full bloom.

Is change an ally or an enemy? It's certainly interesting to note how differently people respond to it. Some can accept shifting circumstances with ease and flexibility, while others resist and create an atmosphere of negativity that impacts their lives and spreads like the flu to those around them.

Exercise #1:

Pinpointing Sources of Negativity in Your Life

What areas in your personal and professional life are contributing to feelings of negativity? Even though you may not consider yourself a negative person, it's helpful to take stock occasionally. As you respond to each question, consider how (or whether) you've had to change because of the particular situation the question addresses.

A. Professional Environment

Downsizing

Yes   No

☐   ☐   Have you been through downsizing in the last three years?

☐   ☐   Did it affect you personally? How? _____

_____

_____

_____

☐   ☐   Did it affect co-workers close to you? How? ____

_____

_____

_____

Team Building

☐ ☐   Is your management fully supportive of the team concept?

☐ ☐   Have changes occurred in your job due to team building? What are they? _____

_____

_____

_____

_____

☐ ☐   If you're a manager, do you feel disempowered because of team building in your operation?

☐ ☐   Does your team pull together?

☐ ☐   Do you have team members who resist the team concept?

☐ ☐   Do you enjoy the interdependence of teams? Why or why not? _____

_____

_____

_____

_____

Skills/Training

☐ ☐   Do you feel qualified to do your job?

☐ ☐   Would additional training enable you to do a better job? What kind of training do you need?

_____

_____

☐ ☐   Do you feel comfortable asking for additional training?

☐ ☐   Do you feel your lack of education is holding you back?

☐ ☐   Would you consider going back to school?

B. Personal

Family Life

☐ ☐   Are you part of a two-income family?

☐ ☐   Do you have a good child care situation?

☐ ☐   Are your children having any school or social difficulties?

☐ ☐   Does anyone in your family abuse alcohol or drugs?

☐ ☐   Does your family spend quality time together?

Sandwich Generation

☐	☐	Do you have any grown children still (or again) living at home?
☐	☐	Do you require them to take responsibility for some of the household chores?
☐	☐	Do you have elderly parents you are responsible for?
☐	☐	Are you able to communicate your needs to both your parents and your children?
☐	☐	Do you allow yourself personal time for things you want to do?

Racial and Sexual Inequality

☐	☐	Are you a member of a minority?
☐	☐	Is your salary less than another, non-minority person doing the same job?
☐	☐	Do you feel your organization is aware of such disparities?
☐	☐	Do you feel additional pressure to excel because you are part of a minority?
☐	☐	Do you communicate your concerns in a positive way to the appropriate people?

Financial Pressures

☐ ☐ Do you work with a budget?

☐ ☐ Are you living beyond your means?

☐ ☐ Do you have extensive debt that prevents you from making a job change?

☐ ☐ Do you have a "rainy day" fund?

☐ ☐ Are you saving sufficiently to pay for your child's education and other necessities?

☐ ☐ Have you planned for your retirement?

Look back over your responses. Are you surprised at the number of changes you've been through? Understanding the changes that have occurred in your life can be helpful in putting things in perspective.

Note: Managers, it is very helpful to look at these areas in relationship to the people who are working for you. What have they experienced in the past three years that may be affecting their jobs?

The Effect of Your Outlook

What would your response be in the following scenario?

Late Friday afternoon, you're called into your boss's office. She acts very nervous, and then says: "I'm really sorry to tell you this, but things haven't been going very well for the company, and I'm going to have to let you go. You've done a very good job, but you just don't have seniority. We're going to try to keep the people that do have seniority with the firm as we ride this out. We'll give you a month's severance and an excellent recommendation, but I'm afraid this is your last day."

Most people have been through drastic situations at some point in their careers, and everyone responds differently. One person will see problems as a challenging though temporary state, while another will view the very same situation as disastrous and quite permanent.

Let's look at some reaction "types." (Remember the old question, "Is the glass half empty or half full"?)

The Optimist

The individual who views setbacks as momentary, brief challenges with the potential for a good outcome is an optimist. Optimists actively look for the positive side of a situation or a person and then move forward quickly to embrace the possibilities.

The Pessimist

Pessimists view change more seriously and, of course, rather bleakly. They tend to give up more quickly, feeling less able to cope with a situation. Challenges may even appear insurmountable, though after thinking things through, pessimists can usually move forward. The pessimistic world view is primarily one of lack and limitation.

The Negativist

The most extreme reaction is that of the negativist. These individuals feel that nothing they do will make a difference. They feel helpless, having little or no control over the events in their lives. No matter what they do, the outcome will turn out poorly, or so they are convinced. When challenged, they give up easily, leaving themselves little opportunity to experience more positive results. Negativists are easily defeated because their view of the world makes something or someone else responsible for interfering with their success.

The outlook you turn on life and the world around you determines how you will respond to people and events that throw you a curve or even just beckon invitingly. Although your view of the world may have been established very early, perhaps in childhood, it can change as your experiences and exposure place you in more positive or negative situations and surroundings.

Although you may not be aware of it, the way you think about things—as an optimist, a pessimist, or a negativist—can have a tremendous impact on the attitude you express and the way you communicate with others. If you always think about how things never work out for you and how you have no control over the results, the average outcome will probably be less than you desire.

For example, consider an employee who doesn't receive a much-anticipated promotion. The pessimist will decide: "I'm never going to be promoted. I don't stand a chance in this company. They will never understand me." This bitter acceptance of a perceived (imagined?) defeat will carry over to that employee's productivity, sales techniques, and so forth. The optimist, on the other hand, reflects *upward*: "I really thought that promotion would have been a good move. My boss must know something I don't yet. There must be something better for me coming up in the future." From this point of view comes new energy and fresh goals.

Your thoughts hold a significant sway over how you respond to situations and how others perceive you. If you're in a slump, you may be unaware of how habitually negative your thought patterns have become. Listen in—is there a pattern in your thoughts?

Exercise #2:

Understanding Your Outlook

If the following situations occurred in your life, what would your immediate thought be about each? Write down your spontaneous response in the space provided.

1. You are complimented on a project you have just completed.

   Thought: _____

   _____

2. Your boss has not spoken to you all day.

   Thought: _____

   _____

3. A co-worker asks to meet with you.

   Thought: _____

   _____

4. You have just been promoted to a job in a department you do not like.

   Thought: _____

   _____

5. You have trouble returning the tennis ball over the net to your partner.

   Thought: _____

   _____

6. Your daughter hasn't called for a week.

   Thought: _____

   _____

7. You receive an invitation to join a prestigious organization.

   Thought: _____

   _____

8. You receive an envelope from the Internal Revenue Service.

   Thought: _____

   _____

Now, go back and review your responses. Do your thoughts about these situations tend to be more negative or more positive/neutral? Look at the ones that are more negative—is there a different way you might perceive those situations (and perhaps to give yourself a more positive outcome)?

two

Friend or Foe?

Do you find yourself "collecting" negative people? It's a good idea to do an inventory every once in a while of who you spend your time with. If you spend much of the day around negative sorts, you may begin to sound like them. It's amazing how quickly we begin to take on mannerisms and speech, both fun and colorful as well as negative and dismissive.

Besides these outward signs, there are subtler effects of spending time around negative people. Do you spend time around anyone who "drains" you? You know, after he or she walks away you feel as if you've put in a hard day's work—and all you've done is have a conversation. These are *toxic* people. They contribute very little (except headaches) but take a lot. How much time are you spending around these noxious types? Give this some serious thought.

An equally important consideration is how you respond to people who are toxic. It may be difficult to answer this question, as it depends on the degree to which the "poison" affects you. If you're able to fend off the negative impact, then it may not be necessary to address the situation at all. If you know what to expect when you're around these people, just stay vigilant about not internalizing their attitude—remain true to your own, more optimistic one. This requires energy on your part, but if the person is significant to you, then it's worth the energy you expend.

Negative people not only come in different sizes and shapes, they also assume various roles and priorities in your life (sometimes changing over time). How you handle them depends on their spot in your personal hierarchy. Some examples follow.

At Work

A Negative Boss

How many times have you looked at your boss and said to yourself, "If only he/she would respond differently, it would be so much easier to work in this office." Unfortunately, most people aren't in the position to just walk away from a job because they have a negative boss. Because most negativists don't accept responsibility for the problems in the office—they'll usually blame them on someone else—*you* have to develop coping strategies (skills) that enable you to coexist with such individuals.

The Curmudgeon. When the Curmudgeon walks into the office in the morning, there's no smile, no greeting. The first thing out of his or her mouth is usually on the order of "This office is a mess. We're behind on everything. It's never going to improve. We'll all probably die in this rubbish pile with nothing completed."

This type of greeting is your signal to put some distance between yourself and the boss. Although this extreme attitude is not particularly catching, you're safer if you treat it as if it were. When your boss is primed for a bad day, his or her ear will be tuned to any statements you make that can be turned into negative ammunition. You and your co-workers may find yourselves the recipients of this boosted negativity later in the day.

The best advice? Keep your distance whenever possible. Limit the number of conversations you have with The Curmudgeon. Keep all interactions brief and to the point. Do not argue. Do not attempt to create a new perspective for this person; you'll only make things worse.

The "Yes, But-ter." Have you ever walked into your boss's office with a "great idea"? One that you know, without a doubt, is going to completely change the way the company does business? You can see yourself being named vice president. Minutes later, though, you've been spun completely around, and now you're picturing yourself sitting on the street corner with a sign saying "WILL WORK FOR FOOD."

The conversation probably sounded something like this:

"I have an idea that I think will change the way we do business. Not only will it give us an opportunity to obtain a larger share of the market, but it will also affect our bottom line and give us a larger profit margin. Here's what it looks like; what do you think?"

"*Yes*, it is a good idea, *but* we tried something like that ten years ago and it didn't work then. And I'm quite certain it won't work any better today."

As deflated as you may feel at that moment, take time to understand what this person is really saying. Stop and ask yourself these questions:

- *Am I rocking the boat?*

    If you're talking to a boss who's nearing retirement, he or she is probably not going to be open to making changes that could jeopardize the time left. In the early stages of your presentation, address any risks you feel could torpedo the outcome you desire.

- *Does this person want to be sold?*

  The boss's resistance may be a test. That is, he or she may want to know just how much thought you've given this concept. How serious are you about developing it further? How much knowledge do you have in this area? If you're serious, then you must sell the idea with all the passion and enthusiasm you can muster.

- *Am I prepared?*

  If you know you're walking into the lair of a "Yes, But-ter," be prepared. Address the negative thoughts before he or she has the opportunity to present them first. Prepare examples of ways your business climate has changed, or how the company has grown. Review the marketplace and the shifts that might affect your concept. Although this strategy requires homework, in the long run you're more likely to reap the rewards you desire.

The Tragi-Dramatic. No matter what, this boss can take the smallest incident and blow it into a major crisis. For example, it's 9:00 a.m. on Tuesday. The Tragi-Dramatic rails: "Do you realize what a disaster you've created? We may never be able to rebuild our relationship with this client. You know they want their status reports by 5:00 on Mondays. How could you have possibly let this happen?" You, however, have already called the client and explained the circumstances. They're fine—no ruffled feathers, no damaged relationship. The boss, though, is too wrapped up in staging a drama to hear your response.

Maintain your calm no matter what. Write a memo afterward outlining the situation and the steps you've taken to correct it. Do not try to interrupt, as this will only create more drama. Prepare to weather the storm until your boss has calmed down.

The Undercutter/Underminer. A boss like this always leaves you feeling as if the ground you're walking on may drop out from underneath you at any moment. As a means of maintaining their own self-esteem, these types regularly undermine the esteem of others. If these bosses can make you feel less competent, you're more likely to turn to them for answers. The Undercutter builds his or her job base at the expense of those around them.

Be aware and beware of this boss. The written word is possibly the most effective tool you can use when dealing with such individuals. If possible, also involve a third party in any major communications. Anytime you feel you've just had the rug pulled out from under you, immediately go to your desk drawer, pull out a mirror, look yourself in the eye, and say: "I'm okay. I'm a competent, honest person. I like myself!" Maintaining your self-esteem will be a challenge sometimes when dealing with this kind of boss.

The Perfectionist. Though not necessarily a negative boss per se, The Perfectionist can certainly create a negative atmosphere. These driven people expect *everything* to be done perfectly, in most cases not only by you but also by themselves. This requirement, of course, is impossible to satisfy.

The most effective way to work with The Perfectionist is to ask questions…*lots* of questions. Attempt to get him or her to clearly define the desired outcome. If you're in doubt about any part of the assignment, ask more questions. Explain, "I need additional information since I want to do this right the first time."

Negative Co-Workers

Although they don't often threaten your professional well-being to the extent that a negative boss can, negative co-workers can nonetheless taint your work environment and make you wish you were earning a living a million miles away.

Moaners and Groaners. You're sitting at your desk, and for the tenth time you hear a co-worker mumbling: "I can't stand this place. I keep telling Ms. Evans that this project is impossible. It's going to take months to finish. Besides, the equipment they've given us to work with is so archaic that no one in his right mind would keep working here." And so it goes, day in and day out.

The first step in dealing positively with the situation is to ask yourself, "Is this person aware of how negative he or she sounds?" Some people grew up with negative dialogue surrounding them all the time, so their comments may sound very natural to them. If you have a relationship with such a co-worker, you may want to speak with that individual on a personal level, pointing out how negative he or she sounds. You might simply say something like this:

"Kevin, sometimes when we're talking, you sound very negative. I don't know whether you're even aware of it— sometimes we don't realize how what we say sounds to someone else. I just thought you'd appreciate my mentioning it."

Remember that you have the right to establish boundaries—whether your relationship is personal or not—letting this person know that you don't want to be a part of a negative conversation:

"Kevin, I understand you're not happy working here; however, I don't feel that way. This job is important to me. When we have these negative conversations about work, I find it begins to affect my attitude. Why don't we focus on finding some positive things around here rather than talking about what's wrong all the time. If we can do this, I think we'll both feel a lot better about our jobs."

Manipulators. The Manipulator sees people as pawns to move about, as in a chess game. These controlling individuals work diligently at creating situations to their liking. One of their favorite tools is instant intimidation, making you feel foolish or like less than you really are:

"Judy, I've been watching you lately, and I question whether you actually understand the seriousness of this project. I think this may be an assignment that should've been given to one of the more senior people. But, since it was given to you, I'll do my best to work with you and try to help you complete it. In order to do this, though, you'll have to make your schedule fit in with mine."

Whoa! Count to ten, and then carefully and assertively explain your perspective on the situation. Thank The Manipulator for the offer of assistance, and let him or her know what you plan to do should a problem arise.

Victims. "Why me? Why is everyone always picking on me?" That's the standard battle cry of the perpetual victim. These people feel stuck in their helplessness and hopelessness and exert no control over a situation (though frequently they're the ones who have set it up to begin with). The following scenario may strike you as familiar:

Several co-workers are sitting around the table in the lunchroom. One of them, Susan, comments about the amount of work she's been doing lately. "Mr. Smith has given me three different reports this week that have to be out by Friday. And I just don't know how I'm going to be able to finish them. I don't know why everyone always gives me all their work to do. After all, I'm not the only person in the office capable of doing this type of work. I just don't think it's fair how Mr. Smith always dumps all the tough stuff on me."

Here's an appropriate response in this case:

"Susan, have you talked with Mr. Smith and told him that you have too much work to do?"

"No, he doesn't care."

"How do you know that? If you don't keep him informed of your workload, he'll just keep on giving you more. Why don't you try talking to him and letting him know what's going on? The situation certainly isn't going to improve this way."

When you hear the wail of "Why is everyone picking on me?" your initial response may be to sympathize. Don't. By sympathizing you only encourage more "poor me's." Listen carefully to what self-made victims are saying, and try to get them to examine possible solutions to the situation. Remember, they're not natural problem solvers, but with your support they may find ways to deal with situations that in the past have made them feel like victims.

Crabapples. You walk into the office in a really great mood, and there is Sourpuss Charlie sitting at his desk. You smile and greet Charlie with a warm, friendly "hello"; he in turn snarls as you walk by. This is a common, everyday occurrence, and yet you find it gets to you and sets a bad tone for the day.

There are two ways to view this situation. You can accept this Crabapple the way he is (and stop internalizing his surly responses as a direct attack on you), or you may want to consider Charlie as one of those people who just doesn't function well in the morning. If this is the case, it's best to just leave him alone until he's able to respond like a human instead of a grizzly bear. You may want to point out to him (some afternoon!) how his response affects you in the morning, and let him know how much you would appreciate a friendlier greeting.

With Friends

Because friendships often have a familial as well as a familiar quality, you may fall into roles with friends that somehow make you think you're being loyal and supportive if you put up with negativity. Well, you can toss that myth into your mental trash compactor right now.

Friends deserve honest feedback from each other—it's the primary insurance policy on your relationship. One way to deal with a friend's negativity—particularly if he or she has a hard time recognizing the tendency—is to develop a signal between the two of you. When one of you sounds negative, the other person gives a special signal as a reminder. Sometimes this simple sort of feedback can significantly modify (or at least curb) negative impulses.

If a situation is more serious, you may find that it requires more attention. Perhaps this is a longtime friend who's become progressively more negative as the years have gone by and is unresponsive to your feedback. You have two options:

1. You may decide to put some distance between you. You need friends who are supportive, not people who drain you and make you feel like you've been pulled through a keyhole everytime you see them.

2. You may want to just establish some personal boundaries. That is, if you wish to continue this friendship, consider how much time you can spend with this negative person without it affecting you personally and then plan your time accordingly. Also, if you plan to spend more of your time with this person in group settings, you don't have to spend as much time one on one. Make arrangements to meet this friend at the movies or to go for a cup of coffee. This limits the amount of time you're spending together but still honors an old friendship.

Exercise #3:

Dealing With Toxic Types of People

A. List the names of the people you spend most of your time around. Which category do they fit in?

Name	Optimistic	Pessimistic	Very Negative	Toxic
1. _____	☐	☐	☐	☐
2. _____	☐	☐	☐	☐
3. _____	☐	☐	☐	☐
4. _____	☐	☐	☐	☐
5. _____	☐	☐	☐	☐
6. _____	☐	☐	☐	☐
7. _____	☐	☐	☐	☐
8. _____	☐	☐	☐	☐
9. _____	☐	☐	☐	☐
10. _____	☐	☐	☐	☐

B. Now match up the people you see as Pessimistic, Negative, or Toxic with the types described in this chapter. Once you've identified those who function as "minuses" in your life, reread and apply the specific strategies discussed for each.

1. *Name:* _____

   Type: _____

   Strategy: _____

2. *Name:* _____

   Type: _____

   Strategy: _____

3. *Name:* _____

   Type: _____

   Strategy: _____

4. *Name:* _____

   Type: _____

   Strategy: _____

5. *Name:* _____

   Type: _____

   Strategy: _____

6. *Name:* _____

   Type: _____

   Strategy: _____

7. *Name:* _____

   Type: _____

   Strategy: _____

8. *Name:* _____

   Type: _____

   Strategy: _____

9. *Name:* _____

   Type: _____

   Strategy: _____

10. *Name:* _____

   Type: _____

   Strategy: _____

three

How Negative Are *You?*

It's easy to recognize negativity in others and criticize them, but it can be quite a challenge to see it in ourselves. It's hard to admit that we may be negative and thereby responsible for some of the negative events that occur in our lives.

First of all, do you consider yourself a positive person? Take a few minutes to answer the following questions as directly and spontaneously as possible:

- Do you have a positive attitude?

- Do you feel good about yourself?

- Do you like who you are and what you do?

- Do you appreciate your own uniqueness?

- Are you confident in the actions you take on a daily basis?

- Do you see yourself as a success?

- Do you feel you have the potential to improve?

- Do you take responsibility for your own actions?

- Do your close friends have a good attitude about life?

Now go back and review your answers. Your positive attitudes are a major source of well-being. There is tremendous power in your mind. How you view yourself—along with the beliefs you have about your capabilities—will profoundly affect the results you produce. For example, athletes who don't believe in themselves will not be the ones who cross the finish line first. The attitudes and beliefs they have about winning become major contributors to the outcomes they experience in their events.

Many athletes use visualization to achieve a more positive outcome. They picture their wins, making their positive attitude come alive. This winning strategy is certainly not limited to professional competitors. Anyone can practice and experience the benefits—with a more positive attitude come more positive results. Empowering yourself and others all begins with you.

The first step . . .

The attitudes you harbor and express are a reflection of your belief system. The beliefs you have about yourself and the events that occur around you create the way you will respond. Many of your current beliefs are the direct result of programming you received as a small child, and they've become the internal rules that direct your life every day.

For example, Frank often says ruefully that he's not good at math. As a result of that belief, he avoids any job that might require even the simplest math. Anytime he is faced with a situation that demands solving a mathematical problem, Frank makes a negative remark regarding his abilities to handle the situation. When he was having problems with math in fifth grade, his teacher said: "Frank, you should never do anything in your career that requires any math. You are just not a mathematician." Unfortunately, he believed that ill-considered remark, and he's never challenged it since.

Or consider the case of Karen. When overlooked for a promotion, her response was one of fear and frustration. She feels that she will never get a promotion because success just isn't within her reach. She believes she was never meant to be successful. She's bought into what her parents had always told her—that only the men in her family have been or could be successful.

Although we outgrow various beliefs as we mature and have new experiences, we don't always let go of them completely, allowing them instead to keep directing our lives. Whenever you come up against an outcome you don't like, ask yourself these questions:

- What is my belief about this situation?

- Do I truly believe this to be the truth today?

- What effect is it having on the consequences I am experiencing in my life?

- Is there a different way I can view this situation that would give me more positive results?

It's not easy to recognize negative beliefs in ourselves—generally most of us prefer the image of perfect, positive individuals. However, if you find yourself feeling incompetent, defeated, and out of control, it's time to do some investigative research on your belief system. An excellent way to begin this process is to maintain a journal of events that occur in your life each day, recording as well your mental response to each situation. Here are two examples:

Event:	The boss took three of my co-workers out to lunch today.
Response:	My boss must not like me. I have trouble getting along with people. I've never been any good at social situations.
Question:	Can you prove to yourself that you're not good at social situations? Or is this a belief that doesn't fit who you are today?

Event:	I had difficulty getting dressed this morning for the meeting with our new client.
Response:	I look terrible in everything. I'm just not very attractive. I've never been able to wear clothes like my sister. She always looks great in everything she wears.
Question:	Who said you're not as attractive as your sister? Do you really look terrible in everything, or just the one black suit that didn't fit this morning?

When you read these examples, did you notice how quickly the response turned into vast generalizations? A belief system that is operating in the negative tends to exaggerate and bend things out of perspective.

Awareness is a big step toward making major belief shifts. Watch for themes and patterns that continually recur. As they do, question yourself:

- What is your belief about this event?

- Is the belief you hold one that enhances your life and builds you into a more positive, capable individual?

The more positive and affirming your belief system, the higher your self-esteem. And the messenger between the two is *you*.

What You Say to Yourself

The conversations you have with yourself can be just as important in coping with personal negativity as the ones you share with other people. Have you ever listened closely to the conversation that's going on in your head?

We all have an internal voice that chatters at us much of the time. Some people even have a full grievance committee telling them what to do and what not to do, how to do it, and when to do it. Perhaps you've escaped the entire committee, but the one voice can be just as powerful. This "critic" can have a tremendous effect on your self-esteem—the way you view yourself—and your overall mind-set, putting you in a positive or negative frame of mind.

Let's look at an example of self-talk and the outcome you can create in an average day. For example, have you ever started out the day by "getting up on the wrong side of the bed"? Have you ever noticed that once it starts that way, things tend to get progressively worse as the day goes on? Does the following have a familiar ring?

Monday morning. Liza wakes up with a start and discovers her alarm didn't go off and she's late to work. She dashes around her apartment trying to pull things together. Her clothing is all over the place, and she finally locates a pair of pantyhose. As she pulls them on, her nail snags and starts a long run down the leg. "This day is already a mess. Nothing is going right!" After locating her keys, she hurries out to start the car and in her frenzy she floods it. This costs her another forty-five minutes. As she's driving to the office, she pictures a full parking lot and knows she's going to have to walk for blocks. And, of course, after visualizing this scenario, she gets to work and can't find a parking place. The day continues to produce one negative event after another. "Nothing ever goes right in my life," she moans.

Do you think there might be something to the concept of self-fulfilling prophecy? Be aware of this the next time you have a day that starts out poorly. Stop, take a few deep breaths, and listen to your self-talk. Change that internal conversation and watch the difference in how your day unfolds. Just because it starts out badly doesn't mean it has to continue that way. You're the one in charge, and you write the script for your internal voice.

Your internal critic is also quite good at producing guilt via lots of "shoulds" and "shouldn'ts." Check out your self-talk in this area. For two or three days, make notes of all the "should" and "shouldn't" statements that your inner voice rattles off to you:

- "Oh, I shouldn't have said that—they may not like it."

- "I should have taken that letter to Mr. Brown's office immediately."

- "I should have told Julie I'd go out with her tonight. I know she's been lonely since she lost her job."

- "I should've called Dad this afternoon."

- "I shouldn't have eaten that piece of cake for dessert. I feel miserable."

Each time you use some variation of the "should" statement, you're telling yourself you're doing something wrong. This criticism many not be founded on reality, but it's your perception of the situation at that moment. Shoulds can become a large stick that you beat yourself up with mentally. If you tell yourself you're doing things wrong all the time, it won't be long until you really begin to believe it. That's the origin of so much negativity.

What happens when your self-talk is more supportive? When you give yourself positive feedback? Talking to yourself in a more positive way can contribute to feeling and expressing a more positive attitude in all areas of your life. Start tuning in purposefully to those inner conversations, and when you hear your critic being negative, stop and ask yourself, "How can I think about this in a more positive manner?" Here's an example:

Critic: "I hate going to work today. I have that miserable project to work on for Mr. Stone. He's so impossible, and I know that whatever I give him will be wrong. He'll find something to complain about."

Alternate: "I'm sure not looking forward to working on that project for Mr. Stone. He can present some pretty big challenges these days. This time I'm going to surprise him and be one step ahead of every request he makes."

The most common statistic about the number of thoughts you have during the course of a day says you have 50,000 of them, 80 percent of which are negative. Do you want to support a statistic like this? Or do you want to be a person who says: "I choose not to live my life like this. I want to be more positive and have an impact not only on my thought process but also on those around me."

Exercise #4:

Developing a Positive Perspective

Set aside some time each week to focus just on the positive events in your life. Give yourself a fine or demerit for every major negative thought you let creep in during that period. Make sure you fine yourself adequately so you'll really feel the impact. For example, stuff a five-dollar bill into a jar for each "infraction," or deny yourself a favorite television show that week. If you do this regularly each week, you'll be surprised at how much more aware you'll be about your negative self-talk. The more aware you are of your negative inner voice, the more quickly you can change it.

four

Toxic Traits and Negative Habits

Besides that smooth-talking saboteur, your inner critic, certain personal traits also can add negativity problems to your environment. For example, are you a perfectionist? A procrastinator? Are there times when you procrastinate because you don't know how to do something perfectly? These traits can most assuredly cause problems for you and those around you.

The Terrible Twosome: Procrastination and Perfectionism

Procrastinators

Why do we procrastinate? Well, for several reasons:

- We don't want to do the project.

- We don't understand how to do it and are afraid to ask questions.

- The project appears too large and we don't know where to begin.

- We're afraid of not being able to do it perfectly.

One of the negative side issues to procrastination—besides the misery you cause yourself—is that, by your own inaction, you often prevent your co-workers from completing their assignments too. Because they may be depending on the portion you're responsible for, this creates hostility and anger in the work environment.

When you dislike the project. If a project is distasteful and not something you want to do, sit down and preplan what steps you must take to get it done as quickly as possible. Break it down into bite-size chunks that each require a small segment of time. When you attempt to handle distasteful assignments by attacking the entire thing at once, just the *thought* of the project becomes grueling and overwhelming. In Anne Lamott's book *Bird by Bird*, she tells a story about her brother having problems with a school report about birds. Her father saw him struggling on the project and told him to take it one step at a time, "bird by bird." Using this strategy, your mountains will become molehills.

When you need more information. People also procrastinate because they don't have enough information about the project. *Ask questions.* It's always better to ask than to proceed without the proper information and then have to go back and redo. No one likes to do things over, but particularly not when a few appropriate questions would have prevented the problem from occurring.

If you're a supervisor and have this problem with staff members, make sure you are very clear with them how you feel about this issue. You might go so far as to say, "I would rather you ask a thousand questions and do something right the first time than fail to ask the questions and have to redo it." By discussing this ahead of time, you'll find your staff will feel supported and much more apt to utilize all their resources.

When a project is too large. Feeling overwhelmed is another regular culprit in procrastination. You look at your schedule and the stack on your desk and cry, "I can't get all of this done!" How many people is your panic going to affect if you don't complete it? The quicker you take hold and sort out your priorities, the fewer people you're going to make unhappy. That monster stack on your desk will shrink much more quickly if you divide and prioritize. Everything facing you right now may be of major importance, but remember this: You can have only *one* number one priority. Select it and move forward.

When perfection is a problem. Finally, when you're afraid you won't be able to do something perfectly, the paralysis of procrastination can result. Anything close to perfection will elude you, though, if you don't get moving. If you need more information, ask questions; if the job looms too large, dice it up. When other people are counting on you to get your work completed in a timely fashion, step into their shoes—how do you feel when you're counting on someone and they're late? Perfection often exists merely in the eye of the withholder—when colleagues need the core information in a report you're responsible for producing, holding it up so you can fiddle some more with the graphics or polish the prose is indefensible. If you're not meeting basic expectations, you're responsible for some of the negativity around you.

Perfectionists

Perfectionists set standards for themselves that are frequently (if not usually) impossible to meet. If you think you might harbor this trait, how high are your expectations? Are they usually possible for you to fulfill? If not, it might be time to look at how realistic your standards are and make some changes. Since perfection is unattainable, why not strive instead for excellence? Set clear, specific criteria up front, before you begin the project, and then do your best to meet them. When you have reached that point of excellence, take a moment and give yourself a pat on the back for a great job. Most of us don't give ourselves a chance to recognize our good work and take credit for it. Put closure on your accomplishments and thus close out any lingering negativity.

It's Just a Habit

Without reflection, you might misread bad habits as negative personality traits. Habits are simply actions that you perform repetitively until they become a natural occurrence. Think about taking a shortcut through a grassy field. The first time you cross the field, the grass is standing tall and straight. But after you've taken that route for several weeks, the grass begins to wear down. Eventually the growth is gone and there's a path in its place. It's easier to walk on the well-trod path than it is to forge through another area of tall grass—you don't even have to think about where you're walking.

The same phenomenon holds true for any action taken over and over, even negative ones—you learn how to do it so effortlessly that it becomes natural, a habit. Your brain is eventually programmed to respond this way automatically.

Many actions you take during the course of a day are habits:

- Always brushing your back teeth first

- Drinking your coffee out of the same mug

- Parking on the same side of the garage

- Putting off the things you don't like to do

- Being late to every appointment

- Blaming others when you don't get your work done on time

- Responding "yes" each time someone asks you to do something

- Keeping your work space disorganized

When you look over this list of examples, you can quickly see how some are harmless while others become destructive. They may also contribute to the negativity in your life. For example, look at the last habit on the list: "Keeping your work space disorganized." If you're always working at a desk that looks like a cyclone has swept through, you may find yourself feeling overwhelmed, unable to find things when you need them, and very negative and defensive about the situation. Some habits are not just inconsequential "shortcuts"; they actively undermine your well-being and add significantly to your pressure and stress.

How do you go about changing a habit? Statistically, it takes three to five weeks to make or break one. Let's look at a sample bad habit—always being late to meetings. This is a behavior (not a trait) that your co-workers don't appreciate and that certainly won't enhance your career.

1. Write a clear description of the habit you wish to change: "I usually arrive at least fifteen minutes late to meetings."

2. Using your written description, write a positive statement about the habit in the present tense: "I now arrive at every meeting on time."

3. Place this affirmative statement where you will see it numerous times during the day.

4. Repeat this statement several times just before going to bed and upon awakening in the morning. Do this every day for a period of three to five weeks.

Exercise #5 provides you with a framework for choosing a habit you wish to change and tracking your progress.

Exercise #5:

Changing a Negative Habit

A. List ten of your more persistent habits. After you've completed your list, consider which of these behaviors may prevent you from being successful. Which of them could create a negative response from the people around you?

1. _____

_____

2. _____

_____

3. _____

_____

4. _____

_____

5. _____

_____

6. _____

_____

7. _____

_____

8. _____

_____

9. _____

_____

10. _____

_____

B. From the habits that you list, select one that you desire to change. Write a clear description of the habit you wish to change:

_____

_____

_____

C. Write a positive statement about this habit (make sure you write it in the present tense):

_____

_____

_____

D. Now, copy your positive statement to a colorful piece of paper—or make it into a poster where you can see it everyday. Be sure to repeat the affirmation every time you see it for the next several weeks. Good luck—it's worth the effort!

five

Between a Rock and a Hard Place

The message in the preceding chapters has been "It's your choice"—you can choose to live in a negative environment and contribute to it with your own negativity, or you can make a conscious decision to improve your personal attitude and your surroundings. You don't have to take giant steps; small adjustments can ultimately have a large impact on your life.

But what if the source of negativity in your life is not something you can change? What if it stems from something like the size of your city or the prevailing weather conditions? When your only option is to temper your reaction rather than to effect change, the dynamics are much different.

Stress

Stress is a fact of life for most people, and thus it's also a common generator of negativity. Though you may not be able to eliminate stress, you can perhaps reduce it somewhat or change your reaction to it. Take a minute to answer the following questions:

- Are you unaware of when you begin to exceed your limits and your stress level increases?

- Do you take on projects you don't have time for because you're not willing to say "no"?

- Do you make commitments to others without first considering how full your own schedule is?

- Do you book your appointments too tightly and then find yourself running late most of the time?

- Do you ignore the signs when you're tired and continue to push until you're exhausted?

If you answered "yes" to these questions, you need to take a minute and assess what you're doing. We all have an optimum level of stress we can work with, both the "good" kind that keeps us invigorated and the "bad" kind that depletes our resources. Finding yourself operating slightly on the edge may work for you very successfully most of the time, but tolerances can change. Start observing your reactions when you're stressed out. At what point are you functioning on a positive and constructive level, and at what point do you step over the line and start feeling overextended and out of control? Discover your boundaries and honor them. Learn to say "no" at appropriate times.

For example, Carol works hard all day in a physically taxing job, and when she arrives home in the evenings she's tired. Her husband's job requires more mental energy than the physical variety, so many evenings he wants to go out to dinner or to the movies. Carol found herself saying "yes" when she was really too tired to leave the house. She became increasingly negative about her marriage and the way her life was going. Finally she became ill. After talking with her physician, Carol realized she was creating this entire situation by not being honest with her husband and not being willing to establish some realistic boundaries.

Take responsibility for your own health and well-being. If you're not already exercising and doing things that offer some release from a high-pressure environment, start now.

Physical Surroundings

Some people live in surroundings that are unpleasant and/or uncomfortable. If that happens to be your situation, what can you do about it?

For example, maybe you live in a large city and would prefer living in the country, but your present circumstances won't allow such a move. You hate the commute you have to make and very often arrive at work tense and in a foul mood. Does it have to be this bad?

Ease the pain of the commute. Go to the library or bookstores and load up with books on tape. Listening to them on the way to and from work makes the time pass pleasantly and gives your imagination a workout. Or study for a course you're taking by placing your notes onto an audiotape.

Make your commute time more productive. Use a cellular telephone to return your telephone calls. Carry a small tape recorder with you to make impromptu notes of ideas and things you must do.

Use the resources of the city to your advantage. What resources does a large city have to offer that you're not presently taking advantage of? Watch the newspaper and you'll be surprised at the number of free concerts, lectures, and functions to choose from if you just take the time to search them out.

Once a month, plan a discovery weekend. Search out new areas of the city you haven't explored in the past. Find new restaurants and shopping areas that will give you a different perspective. Play tourist for a day and pretend you're exploring a brand new place. You may decide you live in a positive place after all.

What if your dissatisfaction and negativity come from the opposite circumstance—a small town? Are you bored and feeling trapped because there isn't enough to do? While you can't make the town any bigger, you can certainly make it livelier.

Organizations. Many national organizations would like to be represented in smaller areas, but don't have anyone to do the legwork. Look for organizations that you have a special interest in, and contact them to see if you can start a branch in your community.

Book groups. Get fellow "bookies" involved in a regular reading discussion group. You can focus on the best sellers or on areas of special interest. This activity gives you an opportunity to socialize with new people at the same time you keep up on what's happening in the literary world.

Volunteer work. No matter what size your city, there are always agencies and programs that need helping hands. No matter what your skills and interests, you can find a match with a group that would gratefully accept your time and attention. Whether it's stuffing envelopes or chairing a major fund-raiser, nothing has the batting average of volunteer work in knocking negativity right out of the park.

Weather and Climate

Are you surprised to see the weather identified as a cause of negativity? Well, if you live in New Orleans but your taste runs to ski sweaters and cold blustery days, probably not. Weather and climate can definitely affect your "negativity quotient."

For example, if you find the weather too cold, you can fight it and stay inside where it's warm but not terribly healthy, or join the others and learn to have fun out in it. Take up skiing, either in the mountains or of the cross-country variety. It's not only very invigorating, but it puts you in a wonderland you've probably never experienced if in the past you've just pouted under a pile of extra blankets.

At the other end of the climate scale, extreme heat can also make tempers and negativity flare. If it's too hot for you, look for *active* ways to cool off rather than just becoming a frustrated heap in front of the air conditioner. Most areas have some form of water sports—river rafting, inner-tubing, water slides, and so on. If you can't swim, take lessons! Swimming classes aren't just for kids.

If it's not heat or cold but gray days that make your negativity soar, then look for ways to put some mental sunshine in your life.

What about flowers? Take classes in ikebana or other styles of flower arranging. This interaction with color and fragrance and texture can offset the gloomiest effects of cloudy skies. As an alternative, perhaps you'd enjoy developing your green thumb with low-light plants in your home or apartment.

Enjoy the companionship of a pet. Even a simple little goldfish can draw you in with its rich hues and flashing movements. Or maybe your interests would fit well with a bird. Not only are they simple to care for, but just listening to your "feathered friends" talk and sing can provide an immense amount of pleasure.

Start a collection of comedy movies. Find films that make you laugh. Look into the archives of old comedy classics and when you find yourself feeling gray like the weather, watch one of them. You'll be elated at the difference these humorous mental excursions can make in your attitude.

Certain People

It's important to remember you can't always impact another person's behavior. Some negative people are as beyond your reach as the weather itself is.

When you're discouraged and find that things aren't working in your life, it's easy to be drawn into the unflagging negativist's way of thinking. However, just as you can with dreary days or inhospitable surroundings, you can apply some basic principles that work quite well in warding off the effects of a diehard negativist.

Avoid participating. Here's an example of defusing the negativist by avoiding participation: A group of co-workers is discussing a change that's going to be made in the shipping department. They've been asked to put together a plan to facilitate these changes. Their supervisor, Tim, is very interested in hearing their thoughts and ideas, and has every intention of putting them to use. The meeting starts on a positive note as one of the workers expresses what a great boss they have: "Tim really cares about our feelings and wants to help us improve our workload."

The negativist immediately jumps into the conversation saying: "You know he really doesn't care about what we think—he's just trying to humor us into thinking he does. We're stuck with these changes whether we like it or not."

If one person in this group agrees with the negativist, it won't be long until the others begin to agree. To break the negative pattern of the conversation, let your response be more upbeat and clearly your own opinion: "I understand what you're saying, but I don't feel that way. I think Tim really cares about the department and wants to make it work better."

When you refuse to participate in a negativist's black view of things, you keep a light shining on other possibilities.

Stay optimistic and let others hear your optimism. It's easy to be pulled down into a bleak mind-set by an indefatigably negative person. If you find yourself in a potentially consuming situation, acknowledge what the negativist is saying:

> "I understand what you are saying..."

> "I hear what you are saying..."

> "I can appreciate your viewpoint..."

Then continue by sharing your own point of view:

> "But in working with Tim, my experience has not been that at all. I find that he's very interested in my feelings and in helping me do a better job."

Avoid arguing with the negativist. Don't try to argue a dyed-in-the-wool negativist out of his or her pessimism. These dark thinkers strongly believe in negative outcomes, and you won't change their minds.

Listen objectively to the negativist's message. Although it may seem the best course is not to listen to negativists, in fact it's important to hear them. They sometimes have valuable knowledge of a situation, and many times are willing to pass information on to you that others may withhold (because it's negative!). Take the time to listen, but avoid getting recruited onto their negative team.

Pose alternative solutions. When changes occur, you'll find the intractable negativist one of the most resistant to the new course. In working through this with negative individuals, take them first to their comfort zone: the worst possible scenario. Have a look at the very worst outcome that could possibly occur, and then begin to rebuild that outcome. By putting him or her at ease in the bleakest possible scenario, the hard-boiled negativist will be more apt to hear your alternative outcomes as you rebuild the situation.

six

The Power of Positive Planning

One of the best ways for you to focus on the positive is to have a plan for your life. Within that plan will come various goals that give you a sense of direction and a set of challenges to move toward.

Goal-directed people tend to come across as very positive, exciting individuals. Inwardly, they're that way too—their self-talk focuses on their great possibilities, not on the negative issues in their lives. Once you're clear about what you desire, you won't have time to dwell on the negatives either, because there'll be more important things for you to do.

The first step onto this positive path is to write clear, concise goals that you can focus your energies on. If you've tried this strategy before but were unable to achieve the mark you set for yourself, ask yourself the following questions:

- Were my goals realistic and achievable?

- Were they specific?

- Were they measurable?

- Did they have a time frame?

- Were they written?

- Were they compatible with my basic values?

For example, a goal written as *"I want to have a good job by the end of the year"* is too shapeless to confront and ultimately fulfill. By contrast, *"I want to have a job as an account executive in the advertising field earning $60,000 a year by February 15, 1997"* gives you a clear target at which to aim. When you hit the bull's eye, you'll know it!

A very important item on the list of questions above is the last one, concerning basic values. You may want to look carefully at yours. Many people who have difficulty achieving their goals discover they're shooting in a direction that's pointed away from their basic values. With this setup, goals aren't just difficult—they're almost impossible to achieve.

For example, if you were to articulate the goal of becoming CEO of a major corporation by the time you're forty-five, but your number one value is family, you've set up some real challenges. That is, to become a CEO will require many long days and nights at work, which will take you away from your family. Understanding this at the outset will help you work through the challenges you'll face to achieve this goal. Having a clear grasp of your top values will enable you to write more successful goals.

To maintain the most positive attitude possible, write goals for every area of your life: spiritual, family, career, financial, health, relationships, and leisure. In order to have a fulfilling life, it's necessary to strive for balance, and you may find little or no balance in your life if your goals are all focused on career. Most workaholics at some point find themselves asking the question, "Is this all there is to life?" They've ignored what gives it richness and meaning. These are people who can ultimately become bitter and negative.

Keeping a clear perspective and maintaining the balance you desire requires focus and concentrated effort. If your work schedule is like most, you're exhausted by the end of the week. When and if you become too tired, you're vulnerable to becoming negative about what's happening in your life. Offering yourself the opportunity to also "play" at life gives your outlook an entirely different dimension. Take on the assignment of writing a specific goal to enhance the play side of your life each weekend for the next six weeks. Before writing, ask yourself the following questions:

- What things do I like to do that I haven't done in a long time?

- What are the things I have always wanted to do, but never tried?

- What are the things that I see in the Sunday entertainment section of the paper that I tell myself I would like to do?

- What could I do that I would consider outrageous?

- What might I try to do that would push my comfort zone slightly?

- What could I do that would make me laugh?

Many of us spend our lives planning for a wonderful future that never arrives. We seem to feel it isn't appropriate to embrace the present—we must hold out for tomorrow. Well, here's some advice: Step into the present, start planning to do those things you've "always been going to do," and watch the altitude change in your attitude. Set goals that will take you out of your daily patterns and begin to stretch your boundaries. The excitement from the challenge you have placed in your life will make you a much more upbeat and excited person. Once you begin to tap into that sense of accomplishment, that sense of being who you fully are, the positive transformations will begin to occur.

Exercise #6:

Setting Goals to Get Started Now

Write goals for yourself in each of the following categories.
State these goals in clear, concise sentences, and establish
realistic deadlines for each. Read your goals aloud each
morning and before going to bed each evening.

Career Goal _____

_____

_____

To accomplish by _____

Family Goal _____

_____

_____

To accomplish by _____

Financial Goal _____

_____

_____

To accomplish by _____

Health Goal _____

_____

_____

To accomplish by _____

Leisure Goal _____

_____

_____

To accomplish by _____

Relationships Goal _____

_____

_____

To accomplish by _____

Spiritual Goal _____

_____

_____

To accomplish by _____

Bibliography & Suggested Reading

Bing, Stanley. *Crazy Bosses: Spotting Them, Serving Them, Surviving Them*. New York: Morrow, 1992.

Briles, Judith. *The Confidence Factor: How Self-Esteem Can Change Your Life*. New York: MasterMedia Limited, 1990.

Covey, Stephen R. *The Seven Habits of Highly Effective People: Restoring the Character Ethic*. New York: Simon & Schuster, 1989.

Laborde, Genie. *Influencing With Integrity*. Palo Alto, CA: Syntony Publishing, 1983.

Lamott, Anne. *Bird by Bird*. New York: Pantheon Books, 1994.

McWilliams, John-Roger and Peter McWilliams. *You Can't Afford the Luxury of a Negative Thought*. Prentice-Hall, 1986.

Robbins, Anthony. *Unlimited Power*. New York: Fawcett Columbine, 1986.

Satir, Virginia. *Self-Esteem*. Millbrae, CA: Celestial Arts, 1975.

Steinem, Gloria. *Revolution From Within: A Book of Self Esteem*. Boston: Little, Brown and Company, 1993.

Tompkins, L. Michael. *The N.E.R.D. Syndrome*. Sacramento, CA: LaGrange Press, 1984.

Wilbur, Ken. *No Boundary: Eastern and Western Approaches to Personal Growth*. Boulder, CO: Shambhala, 1981.

Williams, Redford, and Virginia Williams. *Anger Kills: Seventeen Strategies for Controlling the Hostility That Can Harm Your Health*. New York: Times Books, 1993.

Available From SkillPath Publications

Self-Study Sourcebooks

Climbing the Corporate Ladder: What You Need to Know and Do to Be a Promotable Person *by Barbara Pachter and Marjorie Brody*

Coping With Supervisory Nightmares: 12 Common Nightmares of Leadership and What You Can Do About Them *by Michael and Deborah Singer Dobson*

Defeating Procrastination: 52 Fail-Safe Tips for Keeping Time on Your Side *by Marlene Caroselli, Ed.D.*

Discovering Your Purpose *by Ivy Haley*

Going for the Gold: Winning the Gold Medal for Financial Independence *by Lesley D. Bissett, CFP*

Having Something to Say When You Have to Say Something: The Art of Organizing Your Presentation *by Randy Horn*

Info-Flood: How to Swim in a Sea of Information Without Going Under *by Marlene Caroselli, Ed.D.*

The Innovative Secretary *by Marlene Caroselli, Ed.D.*

Letters & Memos: Just Like That! *by Dave Davies*

Mastering the Art of Communication: Your Keys to Developing a More Effective Personal Style *by Michelle Fairfield Poley*

Organized for Success! 95 Tips for Taking Control of Your Time, Your Space, and Your Life *by Nanci McGraw*

A Passion to Lead! How to Develop Your Natural Leadership Ability *by Michael Plumstead*

P.E.R.S.U.A.D.E.: Communication Strategies That Move People to Action *by Marlene Caroselli, Ed.D.*

Productivity Power: 250 Great Ideas for Being More Productive *by Jim Temme*

Promoting Yourself: 50 Ways to Increase Your Prestige, Power, and Paycheck *by Marlene Caroselli, Ed.D.*

Proof Positive: How to Find Errors Before They Embarrass You *by Karen L. Anderson*

Risk-Taking: 50 Ways to Turn Risks Into Rewards *by Marlene Caroselli, Ed.D. and David Harris*

Speak Up and Stand Out: How to Make Effective Presentations *by Nanci McGraw*

Stress Control: How You Can Find Relief From Life's Daily Stress *by Steve Bell*

The Technical Writer's Guide *by Robert McGraw*

Total Quality Customer Service: How to Make It Your Way of Life *by Jim Temme*

Write It Right! A Guide for Clear and Correct Writing *by Richard Andersen and Helene Hinis*

Your Total Communication Image *by Janet Signe Olson, Ph.D.*

Handbooks

The ABC's of Empowered Teams: Building Blocks for Success *by Mark Towers*

Assert Yourself! Developing Power-Packed Communication Skills to Make Your Points Clearly, Confidently, and Persuasively *by Lisa Contini*

Notes

Notes